NATIONAL
GEOGRAPHIC

T0052335

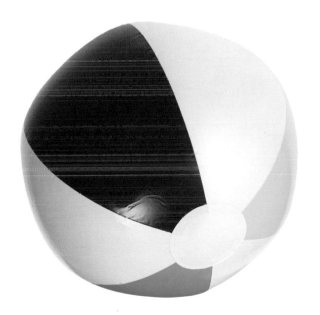

Some
Things
Float

Lesley Pether

Some things float.

Some things sink.

What floats?
What sinks?

4

Will this ball float?

Yes. This ball **floats**.

Will this toy float?

Yes. This toy floats.

Will this rock float?

No. This rock does not float.
It **sinks**.

What will sink?